Simply Sensational™

Barbecue Recipes

GOLDEN WEST PUBLISHERS

ISBN #1-885590-26-1

Printed in the United States of America

Golden West Publishers, Inc.
4113 N. Longview Ave.
Phoenix, AZ 85014, USA
(602) 265-4392

Table of Contents

Marinades

A marinade is a seasoned liquid in which foods such as meat, fish and vegetables are soaked (marinated) in order to absorb flavor and, in some instances, to be tenderized. Most marinades contain an acid (lemon juice, vinegar or wine) and herbs and spices. Because most marinades contain acid ingredients, the marinating should always be done in glass, ceramic or stainless steel containers—never in aluminum.

Barbecue Sauces

Barbecue sauces are brushed on meat during cooking, whether in the oven or on the grill. The special seasonings added to these sauces impart their flavors to the foods on which they are used. Barbecue sauces may also be served as an accompaniment to the meat after it has been cooked.

Zesty Barbecue Sauce

1 med. ONION, chopped
2 Tbsp. BUTTER
2 Tbsp. VINEGAR
2 Tbsp. BROWN SUGAR
4 Tbsp. LEMON JUICE
1 cup KETCHUP
1/2 Tbsp. PREPARED MUSTARD
3 Tbsp. WORCESTERSHIRE SAUCE
1/2 cup WATER
1/2 cup chopped PARSLEY
SALT and CAYENNE PEPPER, to taste

Brown onion in butter. Add remaining ingredients and simmer for 30 minutes. Makes enough sauce for four pounds of meat.

Quick & Easy Barbecue Sauce

1 cup KETCHUP
1 cup WATER
1/2 cup finely chopped ONION
1/4 cup CIDER VINEGAR
2 Tbsp. LIGHT BROWN SUGAR
1 tsp. PAPRIKA
3/4 tsp. LIQUID SMOKE
1/4 tsp. CELERY SEED
6 to 8 drops HOT PEPPER SAUCE

Combine ingredients in saucepan. Bring to simmering stage. Simmer about 15 minutes to blend flavors and thicken slightly. Makes two cups sauce.

Pork Barbecue Basting Sauce

1 tsp. BROWN SUGAR
1 Tbsp. PAPRIKA
1 tsp. HICKORY SMOKED SALT
1 tsp. DRY MUSTARD
1/2 tsp. CHILI POWDER
1/8 tsp. CAYENNE PEPPER
2 Tbsp. WORCESTERSHIRE SAUCE
1/4 cup VINEGAR
1 cup TOMATO SAUCE
1/4 cup KETCHUP
1/2 cup WATER
dash RED PEPPER
dash TABASCO®
1 BAY LEAF
2 cloves GARLIC
1/8 tsp. LEMON JUICE

Combine all ingredients and simmer for 15 minutes. Remove bay leaf and cloves before basting pork.

Hickory Smoke BBQ Sauce

1/3 cup WORCESTERSHIRE SAUCE
2 Tbsp. TABASCO®
2 Tbsp. RED HOT SAUCE
4 Tbsp. BROWN SUGAR
1/4 cup LEMON JUICE
1/4 lb. MARGARINE
1 Tbsp. PREPARED MUSTARD
1 bottle (32 oz.) KETCHUP
1 med. ONION, grated
1 tsp. BARBECUE SEASONING
2 cloves GARLIC, grated
1 cup hickory smoke BARBECUE SAUCE
pinch of GARLIC POWDER

Combine all ingredients in a heavy saucepan and mix thoroughly. Cook for about 3/4 hour, stirring occasionally. Makes 2 quarts.

Honey Spiced Barbecue Sauce

1 1/4 cups KETCHUP
2/3 cup SALAD OIL
3/4 cup VINEGAR or RED WINE
5 Tbsp. WORCESTERSHIRE
1 cup HONEY
2 Tbsp. DRY MUSTARD
3 tsp. fresh grated GINGER
1 LEMON, sliced thin
3 Tbsp. BUTTER

Combine all ingredients in a saucepan and heat to blend together. Makes enough sauce for four pounds of hamburger meat.

Country Style BBQ Sauce

1 cup KETCHUP
1/2 cup CIDER VINEGAR
1 tsp. SUGAR
1 tsp. CHILI POWDER
1/8 tsp. SALT
1 1/2 cups WATER
3 stalks CELERY, chopped
3 Tbsp. chopped ONION
4 Tbsp. BUTTER
4 Tbsp. WORCESTERSHIRE SAUCE
1 tsp. PAPRIKA
dash of BLACK PEPPER

Combine all ingredients and bring to a boil. Simmer abut 15 minutes. Remove from heat and strain. Serve on the side with beef, chicken or pork. Makes 2 1/2 cups.

Poultry Barbecue Sauce

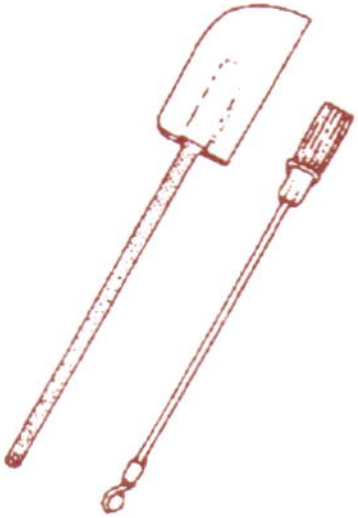

1/2 cup VEGETABLE OIL
1/4 cup VINEGAR
1/4 cup WORCESTERSHIRE SAUCE
1 can (8 oz.) TOMATO SAUCE
2 1/2 Tbsp. minced ONION
2 Tbsp. BROWN SUGAR
1 Tbsp. CHILI POWDER
1 tsp. SUGAR
1/2 tsp. SEASONED SALT

Combine all ingredients and let stand for at least five minutes. Stir before using to brush on chicken or turkey parts or serve on the side. Makes 2 cups.

Teriyaki Barbecue Sauce

1/2 cup TERIYAKI SAUCE
1/3 cup Apricot-Pineapple PRESERVES
1/2 tsp. GINGER
1/8 tsp. GARLIC POWDER
1 Tbsp. CORNSTARCH
1/4 cup WATER

Combine first four ingredients in saucepan and bring to a boil slowly. Combine cornstarch and water and add to sauce. Cook sauce until it thickens. Makes one cup.

Carolina Style Sauce

1 1/2 cups DISTILLED WHITE (or cider) VINEGAR
10 Tbsp. TOMATO KETCHUP
SALT, to taste
Freshly ground PEPPER, to taste
1/2 tsp. CAYENNE PEPPER
pinch of crushed HOT RED PEPPER FLAKES
1 Tbsp. SUGAR
1/2 cup WATER

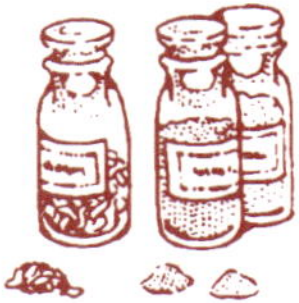

Combine all ingredients in a small saucepan and bring to a simmer. Simmer and stir until the sugar dissolves. Remove from heat and let stand until cool Serve on the side with barbecued meats. Makes 3 cups.

Western Barbecue Sauce

1 cup TOMATO KETCHUP
1 cup BROWN SUGAR
1/2 cup LEMON JUICE
1/2 stick BUTTER
1/4 cup minced ONION
1 tsp. HOT PEPPER SAUCE
1 tsp. WORCESTERSHIRE SAUCE

Place all ingredients in a heavy saucepan and bring to a boil. Reduce heat and simmer for 30 minutes. Serve hot or cool and refrigerate in glass jars or bowls. Makes 3 cups.

Barbecue Sauce Texas Style

3 Tbsp. MARGARINE
1/2 cup diced ONIONS
1 cup TOMATO PURÉE
3 Tbsp. WORCESTERSHIRE SAUCE
1 1/3 cups KETCHUP
3 Tbsp. STEAK SAUCE
1 Tbsp. VINEGAR
1 tsp. LEMON JUICE
2 Tbsp. LIQUID SMOKE
1 1/2 tsp. SOY SAUCE
3/4 tsp. DRY MUSTARD
2 Tbsp. HONEY
2 Tbsp. BROWN SUGAR
1 tsp. ACCENT
1 1/2 tsp. SALT
1 tsp. CHILI POWDER
4 cups HOT WATER
dash of BLACK PEPPER

Melt margarine and sauté onions. Add remaining ingredients and combine. Simmer one hour until sauce is of desired consistency. Sauce may be frozen for later use. Makes six cups.

Lemon-Molasses Barbecue Sauce

1 bottle (18 oz.) BARBECUE SAUCE
1/2 cup BROWN SUGAR
2 tsp. LEMON JUICE
2/3 cup diced ONION
1/4 cup MOLASSES
2 tsp. SWEET HOT MUSTARD

Combine all ingredients and boil until thick, stirring constantly. Makes two cups sauce.

Spicy Poultry Basting Sauce

1 cup ORANGE JUICE
1/2 cup LEMON JUICE
1/4 cup SOY SAUCE
1/4 cup BROWN SUGAR
1 tsp. CURRY POWDER
1 tsp. BLACK PEPPER
1/2 tsp. GINGER
1/4 tsp. MACE

Combine all ingredients thoroughly. Baste turkey or chicken during last 30 minutes of cooking. Makes 2 cups sauce.

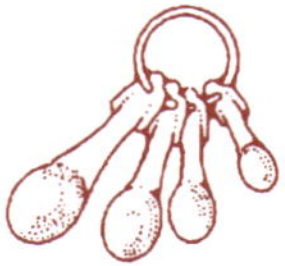

Favorite Barbecue Sauce

1/2 cup OIL
1/2 cup finely chopped ONION
1/2 cup finely chopped CELERY
1/2 cup finely chopped GREEN BELL PEPPER
1 clove GARLIC
2 Tbsp. WORCESTERSHIRE SAUCE
2 Tbsp. BROWN SUGAR
1 tsp. SALT
1/2 tsp. TABASCO®
1 cup KETCHUP
1/2 cup VINEGAR
1/4 tsp. CHILI POWDER
2 tsp. DRY MUSTARD
2 tsp. HORSERADISH
juice of 1 LEMON

Combine all ingredients, heat and simmer covered until all vegetables are tender. Makes enough sauce to baste 4 chickens or a dozen hamburgers.

Low-cal Barbecue Sauce

1 cup fresh LEMON JUICE
2/3 cup APPLE CIDER VINEGAR
2/3 cup unsalted TOMATO JUICE
1/2 cup WATER
3 Tbsp. low-cal BROWN SUGAR
2 tsp. pure GARLIC POWDER
2 tsp. DRY MUSTARD
2 tsp. PAPRIKA
1 tsp. ground BLACK PEPPER
1 tsp. ground RED PEPPER
1 tsp. pure ONION POWDER
2 tsp. RED HOT SAUCE
1/4 cup SAFFLOWER OIL

Combine all ingredients in a saucepan. Heat to boiling. Remove from heat and baste meat or poultry. Makes three cups.

Peanut Butter BBQ Sauce

1 med. ONION
3 cloves GARLIC
3 Tbsp. PEANUT OIL
1 1/2 cups creamy PEANUT BUTTER
1/2 cup BROWN SUGAR
1/4 cup LEMON JUICE
1/4 cup SOY SAUCE
1/4 cup WORCESTERSHIRE SAUCE
1/2 cup BEER
TABASCO®, to taste

Process onion and garlic until almost liquid in food processor. Add peanut oil, peanut butter, brown sugar and process until smooth. Place mixture in a large mixing bowl and add balance of ingredients. Stir until well blended. Makes 4 cups sauce. An excellent marinade and/or basting sauce for ribs, pork or chicken.

Liquid Smoke Barbecue Sauce

1/2 cup LIQUID SMOKE
2 cups KETCHUP
1/4 cup YELLOW MUSTARD
2 Tbsp. CHILI POWDER
1/4 tsp. CELERY SALT
1/4 tsp. GROUND OREGANO
1 tsp. SALT

Combine liquid smoke, ketchup, mustard and chili powder in a blender and blend for one minute at slow speed. Add balance of ingredients and blend at medium speed until thoroughly mixed. Place sauce in a glass jar or bowl and refrigerate. Makes 2 3/4 cups.

Everyday Barbecue Sauce

1 cup KETCHUP
1/2 cup CIDER VINEGAR
1 tsp. SUGAR
1 tsp. CHILI POWDER
1/8 tsp. SALT
1 1/2 cups WATER
3 stalks CELERY, chopped
3 BAY LEAVES
1 clove GARLIC
2 Tbsp. diced ONION
4 Tbsp. BUTTER
4 Tbsp. WORCESTERSHIRE SAUCE
1 tsp. PAPRIKA
dash BLACK PEPPER

Combine all ingredients in a saucepan and bring to a boil. Reduce heat and simmer 15 minutes. Remove from heat and strain. Place in glass bowl and refrigerate up to two weeks. Makes 2 1/2 cups sauce.

Barbeque Sauce for Ribs

3 Tbsp. BARBECUE SAUCE
1/2 cup KETCHUP
3 Tbsp. SWEET & SOUR SAUCE
2 Tbsp. dark BROWN SUGAR
1/4 tsp. CHILI POWDER
1/2 tsp. SALT
1/4 tsp. PEPPER
1/2 tsp. SOY SAUCE
1/4 cup chopped ONION
4 cloves GARLIC, minced
1 tsp. CELERY SEED
1/4 cup RED WINE
1/2 tsp. BASIL
dash GINGER
pinch ANISE SEED

Combine ingredients in saucepan and heat to boiling. Lower heat and simmer 5 to 10 minutes. Baste spareribs while grilling and serve remaining sauce on the side. Makes two cups sauce (enough for 3 lbs. of ribs).

Mushroom Barbecue Sauce

1/4 cup OIL
3/4 cup finely chopped ONION
3/4 cup finely chopped CELERY
1/2 cup diced MUSHROOMS
1/2 cup BROWN SUGAR
1 1/2 Tbsp. prepared MUSTARD
1 tsp. SALT
1 1/2 Tbsp. WORCESTERSHIRE SAUCE
2 Tbsp. CIDER VINEGAR
1 1/4 cups WATER

Heat oil in saucepan. Add vegetables and sauté. Add balance of ingredients and simmer for 30 minutes, stirring occasionally. Makes 1 quart of sauce.

Smoky Rib Sauce

1/2 cup VINEGAR
1/2 cup KETCHUP
1/3 cup WATER
3 Tbsp. WORCESTERSHIRE SAUCE
1/2 tsp. SALT
1/8 tsp. TABASCO®
3 Tbsp. BROWN SUGAR
2 tsp. DRY MUSTARD
3 Tbsp. RED WINE
1 Tbsp. CHILI POWDER
1/2 cup TOMATO JUICE
3 Tbsp. minced ONION
1/4 tsp. GARLIC POWDER
1 Tbsp. PAPRIKA
1 BAY LEAF
2 tsp. LIQUID SMOKE
dash CELERY SALT
coarse ground PEPPER, to taste

Combine all ingredients in a saucepan. Bring to a boil. Reduce heat and simmer, uncovered for one hour. Makes enough sauce for 5 to 6 lbs. of ribs.

Buttery Orange Barbecue Sauce

1/4 cup SUGAR
2 Tbsp. CORNSTARCH
1/2 tsp. ALLSPICE
1/2 tsp. ground CLOVES
1 cup ORANGE JUICE
2 Tbsp. VINEGAR
4 Tbsp. BUTTER

Combine sugar, cornstarch, allspice and cloves in a small saucepan. Slowly stir in orange juice and vinegar. Stir constantly over medium heat until sauce thickens. Boil for three minutes. Stir in butter. Makes one cup sauce.

Old Fashioned Barbecue and Spaghetti Sauce

6 lg. ONIONS, diced
1 cup OIL
6 cans (8 oz.) TOMATO SAUCE
1/4 lb. BUTTER
2 tsp. prepared MUSTARD
1 1/2 Tbsp. MAYONNAISE
1 3/4 cups KETCHUP
2 1/4 cups BARBECUE SAUCE
25-30 drops TABASCO®
3 cups SUGAR

Heat oil and sauté onions. Add tomato sauce and simmer for three minutes. Add remaining ingredients (except sugar). Cook for five minutes, then add sugar gradually, stirring constantly. Cover and cook on medium for approximately two hours.

Steak Barbecue Sauce

1 Tbsp. SALT
1 Tbsp. BLACK PEPPER
1 tsp. DRY MUSTARD
1 Tbsp. TABASCO®
2 Tbsp. GARLIC POWDER
1 Tbsp. grated ONION
1/2 tsp. RED PEPPER
2 Tbsp. PARMESAN CHEESE
1/3 cup WORCESTERSHIRE SAUCE
1/4 cup STEAK SAUCE

Combine all ingredients and stir well. One-half hour before grilling, brush on all sides of steak (or hamburger). Just before cooking, baste again. If desired, baste during cooking. Makes enough sauce for 3 pounds of steak or hamburger.

Fish Barbecue Sauce

1 cup WATER
1/2 cup SOY SAUCE
1/4 cup LIME MARMALADE
3 Tbsp. CORNSTARCH
1/4 cup WATER
1 1/2 tsp. grated LEMON RIND

Add first three ingredients to a saucepan and bring to a boil over medium heat. Stir until marmalade dissolves. Combine cornstarch with water and add to marmalade mixture. Cook until sauce thickens. Stir in lemon rind. Makes 2 cups sauce.

Seasoning & Sauce for Ribs

Seasoning:

- 3 Tbsp. SALT
- 3 Tbsp. SUGAR
- 1 1/4 Tbsp. BLACK PEPPER
- 1 1/2 tsp. PAPRIKA
- 1 1/2 tsp. dry unsweetened LEMON KOOL-AID®

Combine all ingredients and sprinkle on both sides of ribs.

Sauce:

- 1/2 tsp. SALT
- 1 tsp. DRY MUSTARD
- 1 clove GARLIC, crushed
- 1/2 small BAY LEAF
- 1/3 tsp. CHILI POWDER
- 1/2 tsp. PAPRIKA
- 3/4 tsp. HOT PEPPER SAUCE
- 1/2 cup WORCESTERSHIRE SAUCE
- 1/4 cup CIDER VINEGAR
- 2 cups BEEF STOCK
- 1/4 cup VEGETABLE OIL

Combine all ingredients. Baste ribs several times while grilling. Makes enough sauce for eight pounds of ribs.

Chicken Marinade

1/2 cup SOY SAUCE
1/4 cup VEGETABLE OIL
1/4 cup RED WINE VINEGAR
1 tsp. OREGANO
1/2 tsp. SWEET BASIL
1/2 tsp. GARLIC POWDER (with parsley)
1/4 tsp. BLACK PEPPER

Combine all ingredients. Place chicken pieces in a glass dish and add marinade. Cover and refrigerate about 12 hours, turning pieces occasionally. Baste chicken with marinade while grilling.

Bourbon Marinade

1/4 cup BOURBON
1/4 cup SOY SAUCE
1/4 cup DIJON MUSTARD
1/4 cup BROWN SUGAR
1 sm. ONION, diced
1/4 tsp. GARLIC POWDER
dash WORCESTERSHIRE SAUCE

Combine all ingredients in a small bowl, mix well and refrigerate. Use this marinade on all types of meat, chicken, fish, vegetables, etc. Makes one cup of marinade.

Lemon-Rosemary Rub

1 1/2 tsp. grated LEMON PEEL
1 tsp. DRIED ROSEMARY LEAVES, crushed
1/4 tsp. SALT
1/4 tsp. dried THYME LEAVES
1/4 tsp. coarse-ground BLACK PEPPER
2 large cloves GARLIC, minced

Combine all ingredients and rub on beef steaks or roasts. Makes enough to season two pounds of meat.

Southwestern Rub

1 1/2 tsp. CHILI POWDER
1/2 tsp. DRIED OREGANO LEAVES, crushed
1 tsp. GARLIC POWDER
1/4 tsp. ground CUMIN

Combine all ingredients. Rub on beef steaks or roasts. Makes enough to season two pounds of meat.

Spicy Dry Barbecue Mix

1/2 cup CHILI POWDER
1/2 tsp. CELERY SALT
1/4 tsp. each of the following:
- **CURRY POWDER**
- **DRY MUSTARD**
- **dried, finely crushed OREGANO LEAVES**
- **dried, finely crushed PARSLEY FLAKES**
- **ONION POWDER**
- **GARLIC POWDER**
- **WHITE PEPPER**

PEANUT OIL

Combine all ingredients except oil. Brush food to be barbecued with peanut oil and sprinkle with seasoning mixture, rubbing in with fingers or a brush.

Pineapple-Honey Barbecue Sauce

1 can (28 oz.) crushed TOMATOES
2 lg. ONIONS, chopped
5 oz. WORCESTERSHIRE SAUCE
1 can (20 oz.) crushed PINEAPPLE, drained
1/2 cup HONEY
fresh GROUND PEPPER, to taste
3 1/2 cups hickory-flavored BARBECUE SAUCE

Combine all ingredients in a crockpot. Simmer for about five hours.

Barbecued Meatballs

Meatballs:

1 1/2 lbs. GROUND BEEF
1/2 cup MILK
2 tsp. SALT
1/4 tsp. PEPPER

Shape into 16 balls, place in a skillet with a small amount of oil or shortening and brown on all sides.

Barbecue Sauce:

1 cup KETCHUP
1/4 cup WORCESTERSHIRE SAUCE
1 tsp. SUGAR
2 Tbsp. VINEGAR
3 Tbsp. chopped ONION
1 Tbsp. WATER

Combine all ingredients. Pour sauce over meatballs in skillet, cover and cook slowly for ten minutes, turning occasionally.

Barbecued Beef

6 lbs. LEAN BEEF ROAST
1 Tbsp. LIQUID SMOKE
1 bottle (18 oz.) BARBECUE SAUCE
1/2 cup WATER
2 Tbsp. ONION FLAKES
1 Tbsp. PREPARED MUSTARD
1 tsp. LIQUID SMOKE
1 cup KETCHUP
1 tsp. GARLIC SALT
2 Tbsp. SUGAR
dash WORCESTERSHIRE SAUCE

Sprinkle roast with 1 tablespoon liquid smoke and let stand for 20 minutes. Sear roast on top of stove in roaster or Dutch oven. Cover and bake at 300° for 20 minutes. Remove from oven and add 1/2 cup barbecue sauce, water and onion flakes.

Bake an additional 3 hours (or until meat is tender). Remove from pan and shred, slice or cube. Add meat and the balance of ingredients to roasting pan. Simmer about 20 minutes.

Lemon Barbecued Chicken

2 (2 1/2 -3 lb.) broilers, quartered

Lemon Sauce

1 cup SALAD OIL
1/2 cup FRESH LEMON JUICE
1 1/2 Tbsp. SALT
1 1/2 tsp. PAPRIKA
2 tsp. CRUSHED BASIL
1/2 tsp. GARLIC POWDER
2 tsp. ONION POWDER
1/2 tsp. CRUSHED THYME

Place chicken pieces in a shallow glass baking pan. Combine sauce ingredients in a small jar and shake well to blend. Pour sauce over chicken, cover tightly and marinate in refrigerator for six to eight hours; turn occasionally. Brush with sauce, place on grill, skin side up, and grill for 20 minutes. Turn and grill for an additional 20 minutes. Brush often with *Lemon Sauce* while cooking. Serves 4 to 6.

Orange Barbecued Chicken

3 lbs. chicken parts

Orange Sauce

1/2 cup STEAK SAUCE
1/4 cup ORANGE JUICE
3/4 tsp. grated ORANGE PEEL
1/4 tsp. GROUND GINGER

Combine sauce ingredients thoroughly. Place chicken in a baking pan, pierce all pieces with a fork and cover with marinade. Let stand for 15 minutes.

Grill about 45 minutes, turning often and brushing occasionally with *Orange Sauce.*

Note: To bake, place chicken in a single layer, skin side up, in a shallow baking pan. Bake at 350° for about one hour, turning and brushing occasionally with *Orange Sauce.*

Barbecued Chicken & Ham

2 CHICKEN BREASTS, boned
2 very thin slices HAM
2 - 4 slices CHEESE
1 can (4 oz.) diced GREEN CHILES

Beer Marinade

1 cup SOY SAUCE
2 Tbsp. WORCESTERSHIRE SAUCE
1/2 can BEER
1 tsp. POULTRY SEASONING
1 Tbsp. VIRGIN OLIVE OIL

Pound chicken breasts very thin. Marinate in beer marinade for one hour. Layer half of chicken breasts with ham and cheese and sprinkle with chiles. Top with balance of chicken and seal edges with toothpicks. Grill for 15 minutes on each side, brushing often with marinade.

Crispy Chicken Barbecue

1 (3 lb.) CHICKEN, cut into pieces
FLOUR
SALT and PEPPER
1/2 cup OIL
1 can (6 oz.) TOMATO SAUCE
4 GREEN ONIONS, finely chopped
3 cloves GARLIC, finely chopped
1 Tbsp. BARBECUE SPICES
3/4 tsp. CHILI POWDER
1/4 tsp. BASIL
1/4 tsp. CELERY SALT
1 1/3 cups WATER
2 Tbsp. WORCESTERSHIRE SAUCE
dash TABASCO®

Combine flour, salt and pepper and dredge chicken pieces. Brown in hot oil. Combine balance of ingredients in a bowl. Place chicken pieces in a casserole and pour barbecue sauce over all. Cover and bake in 350° oven for one hour. Remove cover during last half hour for crispy crust.

Sweet & Sour Pork Loin

4 to 5 lb. boneless PORK LOIN ROAST, double loin, rolled and tied

Teriyaki Marinade

1 cup BROWN SUGAR, packed
3/4 cup TERIYAKI SAUCE
3/4 cup DRY RED WINE
3/4 cup CHILI SAUCE
1/2 tsp. GROUND CLOVES
1/4 tsp. PEPPER
1/8 tsp. GARLIC POWDER

Combine all ingredients and mix thoroughly. Place roast in a plastic bag and add marinade. Tie bag securely, place in dish or pan and refrigerate at least eight hours, turning occasionally. Drain roast, reserving marinade. Place roast in a drip pan and grill with hood cover closed for two to two and one-half hours. Brush frequently with marinade during last 45 minutes of grilling. Serves 10 to 12.

Orange-Glazed Loin Roast

6 to 8 lb. bone-in PORK LOIN ROAST
1 Tbsp. DRY MUSTARD
SALT and freshly GROUND PEPPER

Rub mustard into roast and sprinkle with salt and pepper. Place roast on drip pan and grill under a closed hood for two to three hours.

Orange Glaze

1/2 can (6 oz.) FROZEN ORANGE JUICE CONCENTRATE, thawed
1/2 cup HONEY
2 Tbsp. STEAK SAUCE
1 ORANGE, sliced

Combine orange juice, honey and steak sauce in a small saucepan. Heat until bubbly. Brush on roast and grill an additional 30 minutes. Baste roast often with sauce. Serve, garnished with orange slices.

Honey Apple Pork Chops

4 (8 oz. ea.) PORK LOIN CHOPS

Marinade:

- **1 1/2 cups APPLE CIDER**
- **1/4 cup LEMON JUICE**
- **1/4 cup SOY SAUCE**
- **2 Tbsp. HONEY**
- **1 clove GARLIC, minced**
- **1/4 tsp. PEPPER**

Combine marinade ingredients and mix thoroughly. Place chops in a shallow glass baking dish and pour marinade over top. Cover and refrigerate at least 8 hours, turning occasionally. Grill chops 40 to 50 minutes, turning and basting with marinade every 10 to 15 minutes. Makes 4 servings.

Hot & Spicy Spareribs

1 rack (3 lbs.) PORK SPARERIBS

SAUCE:

- **2 Tbsp. BUTTER**
- **1 med. ONION, finely chopped**
- **2 cloves GARLIC, minced**
- **1 can (15 oz.) TOMATO SAUCE**
- **2/3 cup CIDER VINEGAR**
- **2/3 cup BROWN SUGAR, firmly packed**
- **2 Tbsp. CHILI POWDER**
- **1 Tbsp. PREPARED MUSTARD**
- **1/2 tsp. PEPPER**

Melt butter in a large skillet over low heat and sauté onions and garlic. Add remaining ingredients and bring to a boil. Reduce heat and simmer for 20 minutes, stirring occasionally. Baste ribs and place, meatiest side down, on grill. (Cover coals with aluminum foil.) Grill over low heat for 20 minutes. Turn and baste. Cook an additional 45 more minutes, basting every 10 to 15 minutes with sauce.

Shortribs Hawaiian Style

4 to 5 lbs. LEAN BEEF SHORTRIBS (cut in 2-inch lengths)

Marinade:

- **2 Tbsp. SESAME SEEDS**
- **1 Tbsp. BUTTER**
- **1 cup SOY SAUCE**
- **3/4 cup RED WINE**
- **1/2 cup RED WINE VINEGAR**
- **4 GREEN ONIONS, diced**
- **1 med. ONION, diced**
- **2 large cloves GARLIC, minced**
- **1 1/2 Tbsp. BROWN SUGAR**
- **1 Tbsp. VEGETABLE OIL**
- **2 tsp. GINGER ROOT, minced**

Melt butter in a large saucepan and add sesame seeds. Cook until seeds are light brown. Add balance of ingredients and simmer until well-blended. Place ribs in a shallow glass dish. Pour marinade over ribs, cover and marinate for at least 8 hours. Barbecue over low flame, turning and brushing with sauce occasionally.

Spareribs with Curry Sauce

12 lbs. SPARERIBS, cut into
2 bone sections
2 cans BEER
SALT and PEPPER

Curry Sauce

1 cup HONEY
1 cup APPLE CIDER VINEGAR
1 cup PREPARED MUSTARD
1 cup APRICOT JAM
1 tsp. POWDERED GINGER
2 Tbsp. CURRY POWDER
1 ONION, finely minced

Place ribs in shallow baking pan. Cover and bake in 325° oven for three hours. After 45 minutes, pour beer over ribs. Half an hour later, salt and pepper lightly, and baste with *Curry Sauce.* Continue basting occasionally until ribs are done. Pan drippings may be thickened for gravy.

Barbecued Shrimp Kabobs

1 lb. SHRIMP
1 can (20 oz.) PINEAPPLE CHUNKS, drained
12 slices BACON, cut in half
8 oz. fresh MUSHROOMS
2 med. GREEN BELL PEPPERS, cut into chunks

Marinade:

1/4 cup SOY SAUCE
1/4 cup SALAD OIL
1/4 cup LEMON JUICE
1/4 cup chopped PARSLEY
dash PEPPER
1/2 tsp. SALT

Combine marinade ingredients, add shrimp and let stand for 30 minutes, turning once. Fry bacon until cooked but not crisp. Alternate shrimp, pineapple, mushrooms, peppers and bacon on skewers. Baste with marinade and grill for six minutes. Turn and grill for four to six minutes longer, basting occasionally.

Grilled Salmon

4 (1-inch thick) SALMON STEAKS
OLIVE OIL
freshly ground PEPPER
2 lg. cloves GARLIC, crushed
1 Tbsp. DRIED DILL
Juice of 1 LEMON

Wipe fish dry. Brush both sides of steaks with oil, then rub surface with garlic. Sprinkle with pepper, dill, and one-half of the lemon juice. Grill 7-8 minutes on each side. Sprinkle with remaining lemon juice and serve. Makes 4 servings.

Marinated Barbecue Chuck Steak

2 to 3 lbs. CHUCK STEAK

Marinade:

1/3 cup OLIVE OIL
1 Tbsp. CHILI POWDER
2 tsp. GROUND GINGER
1 tsp. SALT
2 Tbsp. minced ONIONS
1/4 cup LEMON JUICE

Combine all marinade ingredients. Pour over steak, coating on both sides. Remove steak and grill 8 to 10 minutes on each side. Baste with marinade while cooking.

Marinated London Broil

1 1/2 lbs. FLANK STEAK
1/2 cup STEAK SAUCE
4 tsp. LEMON JUICE
2 tsp. WORCESTERSHIRE SAUCE
1/4 tsp. SALT

Prick steak several times on both sides with fork tines and place in a shallow glass pan. Combine balance of ingredients and pour over steak. Marinate for one hour. Grill 10 to 15 minutes, turning and brushing often with marinade. Serves 4 to 6.

Chuck Roast with Bourbon Sauce

5 to 6 lb. ROAST

Bourbon Sauce

1 bottle (5 oz.) SOY SAUCE
1 Tbsp. WORCESTERSHIRE SAUCE
Juice of 1 LEMON
1/4 cup BROWN SUGAR
1/2 cup BOURBON
1 1/2 cups WATER

Combine all sauce ingredients. Place roast in sauce and refrigerate for 8 to 12 hours. Broil roast over very low heat for one hour (roast will be rare), turning every 15 minutes. Brush with marinade each time you turn roast.

Tropical Chicken

6 CHICKEN BREAST HALVES, boned and skinned

Marinade:

1/3 cup PINEAPPLE JUICE
1 Tbsp. VEGETABLE OIL
1 tsp. SALT
1 tsp. GROUND GINGER
1/4 tsp. GROUND TURMERIC
1/2 tsp. dried THYME LEAVES, crushed
1/4 tsp. HOT RED PEPPER FLAKES, crushed

Combine all marinade ingredients in a large glass dish and whisk until well blended. Rinse chicken with cold water and pat dry. Add chicken to marinade, place in refrigerator for two to four hours, turning several times. Grill, turning once and basting occasionally with marinade until chicken is white throughout and still juicy. (About 8 minutes per side).

Spareribs with Maple Syrup Sauce

6 to 8 lbs. lean SPARERIBS

Sauce:

1 cup MAPLE SYRUP
1 cup KETCHUP
1/4 cup VINEGAR
2 Tbsp. WORCESTERSHIRE SAUCE
4 tsp. ONION SALT
1 tsp. CHILI POWDER
2 tsp. DRY MUSTARD

Divide ribs into 2-rib sections. Blend together sauce ingredients and brush onto spareribs. Arrange ribs in a single layer in a shallow baking pan. Cover and bake at 375° for 45 minutes. Uncover and continue baking about one hour, or until ribs are tender. Brush occasionally with sauce during baking. Serves 10.

Sweet n' Sour Cole Slaw

1 med. CABBAGE
1 med. ONION, sliced
2 CARROTS, sliced
2 GREEN BELL PEPPERS, sliced
SALT and PEPPER to taste
1 cup VINEGAR
1 cup SUGAR
1 cup SALAD OIL

Slice all vegetables very thin. Mix vegetables together and season with salt and pepper. Add balance of ingredients, mixing thoroughly. Serves 10.

Hot Potato Salad

1/2 tsp. POWDERED MUSTARD
1/2 tsp. WATER
1 Tbsp. BUTTER
1 Tbsp. FLOUR
1/2 tsp. SALT
1 tsp. SUGAR
1/8 tsp. ground BLACK PEPPER
1/2 cup WATER
1/2 cup TARRAGON VINEGAR
1 large EGG YOLK, beaten
6 cups hot, sliced POTATOES
2 Tbsp. finely chopped ONION
2 large EGGS, hard-cooked, diced
1 cup diced CELERY
sliced STUFFED OLIVES

Combine mustard and water and set aside for 10 minutes. Melt butter and stir in flour, salt, sugar and pepper until smooth. Gradually add 1/2 cup water and vinegar. Stir a little of the hot mixture into the beaten egg yolk and add back into vinegar mixture. Cook for one minute. Remove from heat, combine potatoes, onions, eggs and mustard in a bowl. Pour hot sauce over all and toss lightly. Add celery & olives. Serves 8.

Cold Potato Salad

4 POTATOES
1/2 cup chopped CELERY
1/3 cup chopped ONION
3/4 cup MAYONNAISE
1/4 cup MILK
1 tsp. SALT
1/4 tsp. ground BLACK PEPPER
1 Tbsp. chopped PARSLEY
3 EGGS, hard cooked, diced

Peel potatoes and cut into halves. Simmer until tender (about 20 minutes). Combine balance of ingredients in a bowl. When potatoes are done, cut into chunks and add to celery mixture. Chill thoroughly before serving. Serves 4 to 6.

Barbecued Corn-on-the-Cob

unhusked CORN on the COB

Soak corn in cold, salted water for 2 hours. Place over hot grill and roast until husks are browned. Serve with butter, margarine, or *Seasoned Butters* below.

Seasoned Butters

Combine one-half cup (one stick) softened butter with your choice of the following:

- **1/2 tsp. CHILI POWDER**
- **1/2 tsp. HICKORY SMOKED SALT**
- **1 tsp. chopped CHIVES**
- **1 tsp. HERB SEASONING**

Makes enough seasoned butter for six to eight ears of corn.

Vegetable Bundles

Place any of the following vegetables on heavy-duty foil (12-inch squares). Season and dot with butter. Use a double fold at top and ends to secure bundle. Grill over medium heat as indicated:

- **Medium, whole MUSHROOMS: 10 to 12 minutes**
- **CARROTS and ZUCCHINI (sliced diagonally): 25 minutes**
- **UNPEELED POTATOES (sliced): 30 minutes**
- **GREEN BELL PEPPER (cut in strips): 30 minutes**

Foil-Baked Apples

4 med. COOKING APPLES, cored
2 tsp. BUTTER (or margarine)
1/2 cup BROWN SUGAR
1/2 cup RAISINS
WATER

Cut about one inch of peel from the top of each apple. Stand each apple in a piece of heavy-duty foil (or double layer of regular strength foil) large enough to cover each apple completely.

Fill each apple core with 1/2 teaspoon butter, 1 to 2 tablespoons brown sugar, and a sprinkle of raisins. Bring corners of foil together on apples and spoon 1 1/2 tsp. of water into each packet. Seal edges securely. Place apples around edge of coals and rotate two or three times during 45 minute baking period.